THIS BOOK BELONGS TO:

CONTACT INFORMATION	
NAME	
ADDRESS	
PHONE #	
EMAIL	

DEDICATION

This Photography Logbook is dedicated to photographers who want to keep track of their photo settings and record the data for future reference.

You are my inspiration for producing this book and I'm honored to be a part of capturing the special moments of your photography journey and documenting your experience.

HOW TO USE THIS BOOK

This Photography Logbook will allow you to accurately record every detail of your photoshoots. It's a great way to record camera setting details, lighting, weather conditions, and more.

Here are examples of information for you to fill in and write the details about your experience in this book.

Fill in the following information:

1. Date and Time - Record date, time of the photo session.

2. Image # - Record the image number.

3. Shooting Mode - Record ISO, WB, aperture, shutter speed, tripod use.

4. Meter Mode - Record EV +/-, lenses, focal length, flash and flash settings.

5. In-Camera Settings - Record specific settings for your camera.

6. Weather - Record weather conditions.

7. Lighting Description - Document the lighting conditions.

8. Props Used - Note any props used in the photo.

9. Notes - A place to write important notes such as the purpose of the photoshoot, backdrops, scenery, photoshoot attendees, etc.

PHOTOGRAPHY LOG

DATE		TIME		○ AM ○ PM
IMAGE #				

SHOOTING MODE		METER MODE		
ISO		EV +/–		
WB		LENS		V R ○ ON ○ OFF
APERTURE		FOCAL LENGTH		
SHUTTER SPEED		FLASH	○ YES ○ NO	
TRIPOD	○ YES ○ NO	FLASH SETTINGS		

IN CAMERA SETTINGS	WEATHER

LIGHTING DESCRIPTION

PROPS USED	NOTES

PHOTOGRAPHY LOG

DATE		TIME		○ AM ○ PM
IMAGE #				

SHOOTING MODE		METER MODE		
ISO		EV +/-		
WB		LENS		V R — ○ ON ○ OFF
APERTURE		FOCAL LENGTH		
SHUTTER SPEED		FLASH	○ YES ○ NO	
TRIPOD	○ YES ○ NO	FLASH SETTINGS		

IN CAMERA SETTINGS	WEATHER

LIGHTING DESCRIPTION

PROPS USED	NOTES

PHOTOGRAPHY LOG

DATE		TIME		○ AM ○ PM
IMAGE #				

SHOOTING MODE		METER MODE			
ISO		EV +/-			
WB		LENS		V R	○ ON ○ OFF
APERTURE		FOCAL LENGTH			
SHUTTER SPEED		FLASH	○ YES ○ NO		
TRIPOD	○ YES ○ NO	FLASH SETTINGS			

IN CAMERA SETTINGS	WEATHER

LIGHTING DESCRIPTION

PROPS USED	NOTES

PHOTOGRAPHY LOG

DATE		TIME		○ AM ○ PM
IMAGE #				

SHOOTING MODE		METER MODE	
ISO		EV +/-	
WB		LENS	V R ○ ON ○ OFF
APERTURE		FOCAL LENGTH	
SHUTTER SPEED		FLASH	○ YES ○ NO
TRIPOD	○ YES ○ NO	FLASH SETTINGS	

IN CAMERA SETTINGS	WEATHER

LIGHTING DESCRIPTION

PROPS USED	NOTES

PHOTOGRAPHY LOG

DATE		TIME		○ AM ○ PM
IMAGE #				

SHOOTING MODE		METER MODE		
ISO		EV +/-		
WB		LENS		V R ○ ON ○ OFF
APERTURE		FOCAL LENGTH		
SHUTTER SPEED		FLASH	○ YES ○ NO	
TRIPOD	○ YES ○ NO	FLASH SETTINGS		

IN CAMERA SETTINGS	WEATHER

LIGHTING DESCRIPTION

PROPS USED	NOTES

PHOTOGRAPHY LOG

DATE		TIME		○ AM ○ PM
IMAGE #				

SHOOTING MODE		METER MODE		
ISO		EV +/−		
WB		LENS		V R ○ ON ○ OFF
APERTURE		FOCAL LENGTH		
SHUTTER SPEED		FLASH	○ YES ○ NO	
TRIPOD	○ YES ○ NO	FLASH SETTINGS		

IN CAMERA SETTINGS	WEATHER

LIGHTING DESCRIPTION

PROPS USED	NOTES

PHOTOGRAPHY LOG

DATE		TIME		○ AM ○ PM
IMAGE #				

SHOOTING MODE		METER MODE		
ISO		EV +/-		
WB		LENS		V R ○ ON ○ OFF
APERTURE		FOCAL LENGTH		
SHUTTER SPEED		FLASH	○ YES ○ NO	
TRIPOD	○ YES ○ NO	FLASH SETTINGS		

IN CAMERA SETTINGS	WEATHER

LIGHTING DESCRIPTION

PROPS USED	NOTES

PHOTOGRAPHY LOG

DATE		TIME		○ AM ○ PM
IMAGE #				

SHOOTING MODE		METER MODE			
ISO		EV +/-			
WB		LENS		V R	○ ON ○ OFF
APERTURE		FOCAL LENGTH			
SHUTTER SPEED		FLASH	○ YES ○ NO		
TRIPOD	○ YES ○ NO	FLASH SETTINGS			

IN CAMERA SETTINGS	WEATHER

LIGHTING DESCRIPTION

PROPS USED	NOTES

PHOTOGRAPHY LOG

DATE		TIME		○ AM ○ PM
IMAGE #				

SHOOTING MODE		METER MODE	
ISO		EV +/-	
WB		LENS	V R ○ ON ○ OFF
APERTURE		FOCAL LENGTH	
SHUTTER SPEED		FLASH	○ YES ○ NO
TRIPOD	○ YES ○ NO	FLASH SETTINGS	

IN CAMERA SETTINGS	WEATHER

LIGHTING DESCRIPTION

PROPS USED	NOTES

PHOTOGRAPHY LOG

DATE		TIME		○ AM ○ PM
IMAGE #				

SHOOTING MODE		METER MODE	
ISO		EV +/-	
WB		LENS	V R ○ ON ○OFF
APERTURE		FOCAL LENGTH	
SHUTTER SPEED		FLASH	○ YES ○ NO
TRIPOD	○ YES ○ NO	FLASH SETTINGS	

IN CAMERA SETTINGS	WEATHER

LIGHTING DESCRIPTION

PROPS USED	NOTES

PHOTOGRAPHY LOG

DATE		TIME		○ AM ○ PM
IMAGE #				

SHOOTING MODE		METER MODE		
ISO		EV +/−		
WB		LENS		V R ○ ON ○ OFF
APERTURE		FOCAL LENGTH		
SHUTTER SPEED		FLASH	○ YES ○ NO	
TRIPOD	○ YES ○ NO	FLASH SETTINGS		

IN CAMERA SETTINGS	WEATHER

LIGHTING DESCRIPTION

PROPS USED	NOTES

PHOTOGRAPHY LOG

DATE		TIME		○ AM ○ PM
IMAGE #				

SHOOTING MODE		METER MODE			
ISO		EV +/-			
WB		LENS		V R	○ ON ○ OFF
APERTURE		FOCAL LENGTH			
SHUTTER SPEED		FLASH	○ YES ○ NO		
TRIPOD	○ YES ○ NO	FLASH SETTINGS			

IN CAMERA SETTINGS	WEATHER

LIGHTING DESCRIPTION

PROPS USED	NOTES

PHOTOGRAPHY LOG

DATE		TIME		○ AM ○ PM
IMAGE #				

SHOOTING MODE		METER MODE	
ISO		EV +/-	
WB		LENS	V R ○ ON ○ OFF
APERTURE		FOCAL LENGTH	
SHUTTER SPEED		FLASH	○ YES ○ NO
TRIPOD	○ YES ○ NO	FLASH SETTINGS	

IN CAMERA SETTINGS	WEATHER

LIGHTING DESCRIPTION

PROPS USED	NOTES

PHOTOGRAPHY LOG

DATE		TIME		○ AM ○ PM
IMAGE #				

SHOOTING MODE		METER MODE			
ISO		EV +/-			
WB		LENS		V R	○ ON ○ OFF
APERTURE		FOCAL LENGTH			
SHUTTER SPEED		FLASH	○ YES ○ NO		
TRIPOD	○ YES ○ NO	FLASH SETTINGS			

IN CAMERA SETTINGS	WEATHER

LIGHTING DESCRIPTION

PROPS USED	NOTES

PHOTOGRAPHY LOG

DATE		TIME	○ AM ○ PM
IMAGE #			

SHOOTING MODE		METER MODE	
ISO		EV +/-	
WB		LENS	V R ○ ON ○ OFF
APERTURE		FOCAL LENGTH	
SHUTTER SPEED		FLASH	○ YES ○ NO
TRIPOD	○ YES ○ NO	FLASH SETTINGS	

IN CAMERA SETTINGS	WEATHER

LIGHTING DESCRIPTION

PROPS USED	NOTES

PHOTOGRAPHY LOG

DATE		TIME		○ AM ○ PM
IMAGE #				

SHOOTING MODE		METER MODE			
ISO		EV +/-			
WB		LENS		V R	○ ON ○ OFF
APERTURE		FOCAL LENGTH			
SHUTTER SPEED		FLASH	○ YES ○ NO		
TRIPOD	○ YES ○ NO	FLASH SETTINGS			

IN CAMERA SETTINGS	WEATHER

LIGHTING DESCRIPTION

PROPS USED	NOTES

PHOTOGRAPHY LOG

DATE		TIME		○ AM ○ PM
IMAGE #				

SHOOTING MODE		METER MODE			
ISO		EV +/-			
WB		LENS		V R	○ ON ○ OFF
APERTURE		FOCAL LENGTH			
SHUTTER SPEED		FLASH	○ YES ○ NO		
TRIPOD	○ YES ○ NO	FLASH SETTINGS			

IN CAMERA SETTINGS	WEATHER

LIGHTING DESCRIPTION

PROPS USED	NOTES

PHOTOGRAPHY LOG

DATE		TIME		○ AM ○ PM
IMAGE #				

SHOOTING MODE		METER MODE	
ISO		EV +/-	
WB		LENS	V R ○ ON ○ OFF
APERTURE		FOCAL LENGTH	
SHUTTER SPEED		FLASH	○ YES ○ NO
TRIPOD	○ YES ○ NO	FLASH SETTINGS	

IN CAMERA SETTINGS	WEATHER

LIGHTING DESCRIPTION

PROPS USED	NOTES

PHOTOGRAPHY LOG

DATE		TIME		○ AM ○ PM
IMAGE #				

SHOOTING MODE		METER MODE	
ISO		EV +/-	
WB		LENS	V R ○ ON ○ OFF
APERTURE		FOCAL LENGTH	
SHUTTER SPEED		FLASH	○ YES ○ NO
TRIPOD	○ YES ○ NO	FLASH SETTINGS	

IN CAMERA SETTINGS	WEATHER

LIGHTING DESCRIPTION

PROPS USED	NOTES

PHOTOGRAPHY LOG

DATE		TIME		○ AM ○ PM
IMAGE #				

SHOOTING MODE		METER MODE			
ISO		EV +/-			
WB		LENS		V R	○ ON ○ OFF
APERTURE		FOCAL LENGTH			
SHUTTER SPEED		FLASH	○ YES ○ NO		
TRIPOD	○ YES ○ NO	FLASH SETTINGS			

IN CAMERA SETTINGS	WEATHER

LIGHTING DESCRIPTION

PROPS USED	NOTES

PHOTOGRAPHY LOG

DATE		TIME		○ AM ○ PM
IMAGE #				

SHOOTING MODE		METER MODE		
ISO		EV +/-		
WB		LENS		V R · ○ ON ○ OFF
APERTURE		FOCAL LENGTH		
SHUTTER SPEED		FLASH	○ YES ○ NO	
TRIPOD	○ YES ○ NO	FLASH SETTINGS		

IN CAMERA SETTINGS	WEATHER

LIGHTING DESCRIPTION

PROPS USED	NOTES

PHOTOGRAPHY LOG

DATE		TIME		○ AM ○ PM
IMAGE #				

SHOOTING MODE		METER MODE		
ISO		EV +/-		
WB		LENS		V R — ○ ON ○ OFF
APERTURE		FOCAL LENGTH		
SHUTTER SPEED		FLASH	○ YES ○ NO	
TRIPOD	○ YES ○ NO	FLASH SETTINGS		

IN CAMERA SETTINGS	WEATHER

LIGHTING DESCRIPTION

PROPS USED	NOTES

PHOTOGRAPHY LOG

DATE		TIME		○ AM ○ PM
IMAGE #				

SHOOTING MODE		METER MODE		
ISO		EV +/-		
WB		LENS		V R ○ ON ○ OFF
APERTURE		FOCAL LENGTH		
SHUTTER SPEED		FLASH	○ YES ○ NO	
TRIPOD	○ YES ○ NO	FLASH SETTINGS		

IN CAMERA SETTINGS	WEATHER

LIGHTING DESCRIPTION

PROPS USED	NOTES

PHOTOGRAPHY LOG

DATE		TIME		○ AM ○ PM
IMAGE #				

SHOOTING MODE		METER MODE	
ISO		EV +/-	
WB		LENS	V R ○ ON ○ OFF
APERTURE		FOCAL LENGTH	
SHUTTER SPEED		FLASH	○ YES ○ NO
TRIPOD	○ YES ○ NO	FLASH SETTINGS	

IN CAMERA SETTINGS	WEATHER

LIGHTING DESCRIPTION

PROPS USED	NOTES

PHOTOGRAPHY LOG

DATE		TIME		○ AM ○ PM
IMAGE #				

SHOOTING MODE		METER MODE		
ISO		EV +/-		
WB		LENS		V R ○ ON ○ OFF
APERTURE		FOCAL LENGTH		
SHUTTER SPEED		FLASH	○ YES ○ NO	
TRIPOD	○ YES ○ NO	FLASH SETTINGS		

IN CAMERA SETTINGS	WEATHER

LIGHTING DESCRIPTION

PROPS USED	NOTES

PHOTOGRAPHY LOG

DATE		TIME		○ AM ○ PM
IMAGE #				

SHOOTING MODE		METER MODE		
ISO		EV +/−		
WB		LENS		V R ○ ON ○ OFF
APERTURE		FOCAL LENGTH		
SHUTTER SPEED		FLASH	○ YES ○ NO	
TRIPOD	○ YES ○ NO	FLASH SETTINGS		

IN CAMERA SETTINGS	WEATHER

LIGHTING DESCRIPTION

PROPS USED	NOTES

PHOTOGRAPHY LOG

DATE		TIME		○ AM ○ PM
IMAGE #				

SHOOTING MODE		METER MODE			
ISO		EV +/-			
WB		LENS		V R	○ ON ○ OFF
APERTURE		FOCAL LENGTH			
SHUTTER SPEED		FLASH	○ YES ○ NO		
TRIPOD	○ YES ○ NO	FLASH SETTINGS			

IN CAMERA SETTINGS	WEATHER

LIGHTING DESCRIPTION

PROPS USED	NOTES

PHOTOGRAPHY LOG

DATE		TIME		○ AM ○ PM
IMAGE #				

SHOOTING MODE		METER MODE		
ISO		EV +/-		
WB		LENS		V R ○ ON ○ OFF
APERTURE		FOCAL LENGTH		
SHUTTER SPEED		FLASH	○ YES ○ NO	
TRIPOD	○ YES ○ NO	FLASH SETTINGS		

IN CAMERA SETTINGS	WEATHER

LIGHTING DESCRIPTION

PROPS USED	NOTES

PHOTOGRAPHY LOG

DATE		TIME		○ AM ○ PM
IMAGE #				

SHOOTING MODE		METER MODE		
ISO		EV +/-		
WB		LENS		V R ○ ON ○ OFF
APERTURE		FOCAL LENGTH		
SHUTTER SPEED		FLASH	○ YES ○ NO	
TRIPOD	○ YES ○ NO	FLASH SETTINGS		

IN CAMERA SETTINGS	WEATHER

LIGHTING DESCRIPTION

PROPS USED	NOTES

PHOTOGRAPHY LOG

DATE		TIME		○ AM ○ PM
IMAGE #				

SHOOTING MODE		METER MODE		
ISO		EV +/-		
WB		LENS		V R ○ ON ○ OFF
APERTURE		FOCAL LENGTH		
SHUTTER SPEED		FLASH	○ YES ○ NO	
TRIPOD	○ YES ○ NO	FLASH SETTINGS		

IN CAMERA SETTINGS	WEATHER

LIGHTING DESCRIPTION

PROPS USED	NOTES

PHOTOGRAPHY LOG

DATE		TIME		○ AM ○ PM
IMAGE #				

SHOOTING MODE		METER MODE		
ISO		EV +/-		
WB		LENS		V R ○ ON ○ OFF
APERTURE		FOCAL LENGTH		
SHUTTER SPEED		FLASH	○ YES ○ NO	
TRIPOD	○ YES ○ NO	FLASH SETTINGS		

IN CAMERA SETTINGS	WEATHER

LIGHTING DESCRIPTION

PROPS USED	NOTES

PHOTOGRAPHY LOG

DATE		TIME		○ AM ○ PM
IMAGE #				

SHOOTING MODE		METER MODE		
ISO		EV +/-		
WB		LENS		V R ○ ON ○ OFF
APERTURE		FOCAL LENGTH		
SHUTTER SPEED		FLASH	○ YES ○ NO	
TRIPOD	○ YES ○ NO	FLASH SETTINGS		

IN CAMERA SETTINGS	WEATHER

LIGHTING DESCRIPTION

PROPS USED	NOTES

PHOTOGRAPHY LOG

DATE		TIME		○ AM ○ PM
IMAGE #				

SHOOTING MODE		METER MODE		
ISO		EV +/-		
WB		LENS		V R ○ ON ○ OFF
APERTURE		FOCAL LENGTH		
SHUTTER SPEED		FLASH	○ YES ○ NO	
TRIPOD	○ YES ○ NO	FLASH SETTINGS		

IN CAMERA SETTINGS	WEATHER

LIGHTING DESCRIPTION

PROPS USED	NOTES

PHOTOGRAPHY LOG

DATE		TIME		○ AM ○ PM
IMAGE #				

SHOOTING MODE		METER MODE	
ISO		EV +/-	
WB		LENS	V R ○ ON ○ OFF
APERTURE		FOCAL LENGTH	
SHUTTER SPEED		FLASH	○ YES ○ NO
TRIPOD	○ YES ○ NO	FLASH SETTINGS	

IN CAMERA SETTINGS	WEATHER

LIGHTING DESCRIPTION

PROPS USED	NOTES

PHOTOGRAPHY LOG

DATE		TIME		○ AM ○ PM
IMAGE #				

SHOOTING MODE		METER MODE		
ISO		EV +/−		
WB		LENS		V R ○ ON ○ OFF
APERTURE		FOCAL LENGTH		
SHUTTER SPEED		FLASH	○ YES ○ NO	
TRIPOD	○ YES ○ NO	FLASH SETTINGS		

IN CAMERA SETTINGS	WEATHER

LIGHTING DESCRIPTION

PROPS USED	NOTES

PHOTOGRAPHY LOG

DATE		TIME		○ AM ○ PM
IMAGE #				

SHOOTING MODE		METER MODE		
ISO		EV +/-		
WB		LENS		V R ○ ON ○ OFF
APERTURE		FOCAL LENGTH		
SHUTTER SPEED		FLASH	○ YES ○ NO	
TRIPOD	○ YES ○ NO	FLASH SETTINGS		

IN CAMERA SETTINGS	WEATHER

LIGHTING DESCRIPTION

PROPS USED	NOTES

PHOTOGRAPHY LOG

DATE		TIME		○ AM ○ PM
IMAGE #				

SHOOTING MODE		METER MODE	
ISO		EV +/-	
WB		LENS	V R ○ ON ○ OFF
APERTURE		FOCAL LENGTH	
SHUTTER SPEED		FLASH	○ YES ○ NO
TRIPOD	○ YES ○ NO	FLASH SETTINGS	

IN CAMERA SETTINGS	WEATHER

LIGHTING DESCRIPTION

PROPS USED	NOTES

PHOTOGRAPHY LOG

DATE		TIME		○ AM ○ PM
IMAGE #				

SHOOTING MODE		METER MODE	
ISO		EV +/-	
WB		LENS	V R ○ ON ○ OFF
APERTURE		FOCAL LENGTH	
SHUTTER SPEED		FLASH	○ YES ○ NO
TRIPOD	○ YES ○ NO	FLASH SETTINGS	

IN CAMERA SETTINGS	WEATHER

LIGHTING DESCRIPTION

PROPS USED	NOTES

PHOTOGRAPHY LOG

DATE		TIME		○ AM ○ PM
IMAGE #				

SHOOTING MODE		METER MODE		
ISO		EV +/-		
WB		LENS		V R ○ ON ○ OFF
APERTURE		FOCAL LENGTH		
SHUTTER SPEED		FLASH	○ YES ○ NO	
TRIPOD	○ YES ○ NO	FLASH SETTINGS		

IN CAMERA SETTINGS	WEATHER

LIGHTING DESCRIPTION

PROPS USED	NOTES

PHOTOGRAPHY LOG

DATE		TIME		○ AM ○ PM
IMAGE #				

SHOOTING MODE		METER MODE	
ISO		EV +/-	
WB		LENS	V R — ○ ON ○ OFF
APERTURE		FOCAL LENGTH	
SHUTTER SPEED		FLASH	○ YES ○ NO
TRIPOD	○ YES ○ NO	FLASH SETTINGS	

IN CAMERA SETTINGS	WEATHER

LIGHTING DESCRIPTION

PROPS USED	NOTES

PHOTOGRAPHY LOG

DATE		TIME		○ AM ○ PM
IMAGE #				

SHOOTING MODE		METER MODE		
ISO		EV +/-		
WB		LENS		V R ○ ON ○ OFF
APERTURE		FOCAL LENGTH		
SHUTTER SPEED		FLASH	○ YES ○ NO	
TRIPOD	○ YES ○ NO	FLASH SETTINGS		

IN CAMERA SETTINGS	WEATHER

LIGHTING DESCRIPTION

PROPS USED	NOTES

PHOTOGRAPHY LOG

DATE		TIME		○ AM ○ PM
IMAGE #				

SHOOTING MODE		METER MODE	
ISO		EV +/–	
WB		LENS	V R ○ ON ○ OFF
APERTURE		FOCAL LENGTH	
SHUTTER SPEED		FLASH	○ YES ○ NO
TRIPOD	○ YES ○ NO	FLASH SETTINGS	

IN CAMERA SETTINGS	WEATHER

LIGHTING DESCRIPTION

PROPS USED	NOTES

PHOTOGRAPHY LOG

DATE		TIME		○ AM ○ PM
IMAGE #				

SHOOTING MODE		METER MODE		
ISO		EV +/−		
WB		LENS		V R ○ ON ○ OFF
APERTURE		FOCAL LENGTH		
SHUTTER SPEED		FLASH	○ YES ○ NO	
TRIPOD	○ YES ○ NO	FLASH SETTINGS		

IN CAMERA SETTINGS	WEATHER

LIGHTING DESCRIPTION

PROPS USED	NOTES

PHOTOGRAPHY LOG

DATE		TIME		○ AM ○ PM
IMAGE #				

SHOOTING MODE		METER MODE		
ISO		EV +/−		
WB		LENS		V R ○ ON ○ OFF
APERTURE		FOCAL LENGTH		
SHUTTER SPEED		FLASH	○ YES ○ NO	
TRIPOD	○ YES ○ NO	FLASH SETTINGS		

IN CAMERA SETTINGS	WEATHER

LIGHTING DESCRIPTION

PROPS USED	NOTES

PHOTOGRAPHY LOG

DATE		TIME		○ AM ○ PM
IMAGE #				

SHOOTING MODE		METER MODE	
ISO		EV +/-	
WB		LENS	V R ○ ON ○ OFF
APERTURE		FOCAL LENGTH	
SHUTTER SPEED		FLASH	○ YES ○ NO
TRIPOD	○ YES ○ NO	FLASH SETTINGS	

IN CAMERA SETTINGS	WEATHER

LIGHTING DESCRIPTION

PROPS USED	NOTES

PHOTOGRAPHY LOG

DATE		TIME		○ AM ○ PM
IMAGE #				

SHOOTING MODE		METER MODE	
ISO		EV +/-	
WB		LENS	V R ○ ON ○ OFF
APERTURE		FOCAL LENGTH	
SHUTTER SPEED		FLASH	○ YES ○ NO
TRIPOD	○ YES ○ NO	FLASH SETTINGS	

IN CAMERA SETTINGS	WEATHER

LIGHTING DESCRIPTION

PROPS USED	NOTES

PHOTOGRAPHY LOG

DATE		TIME		○ AM ○ PM
IMAGE #				

SHOOTING MODE		METER MODE		
ISO		EV +/-		
WB		LENS		V R ○ ON ○ OFF
APERTURE		FOCAL LENGTH		
SHUTTER SPEED		FLASH	○ YES ○ NO	
TRIPOD	○ YES ○ NO	FLASH SETTINGS		

IN CAMERA SETTINGS	WEATHER

LIGHTING DESCRIPTION

PROPS USED	NOTES

PHOTOGRAPHY LOG

DATE		TIME		○ AM ○ PM
IMAGE #				

SHOOTING MODE		METER MODE		
ISO		EV +/–		
WB		LENS		V R ○ ON ○ OFF
APERTURE		FOCAL LENGTH		
SHUTTER SPEED		FLASH	○ YES ○ NO	
TRIPOD	○ YES ○ NO	FLASH SETTINGS		

IN CAMERA SETTINGS	WEATHER

LIGHTING DESCRIPTION

PROPS USED	NOTES

PHOTOGRAPHY LOG

DATE		TIME		○ AM ○ PM
IMAGE #				

SHOOTING MODE		METER MODE	
ISO		EV +/-	
WB		LENS	V R ○ ON ○ OFF
APERTURE		FOCAL LENGTH	
SHUTTER SPEED		FLASH	○ YES ○ NO
TRIPOD	○ YES ○ NO	FLASH SETTINGS	

IN CAMERA SETTINGS	WEATHER

LIGHTING DESCRIPTION

PROPS USED	NOTES

PHOTOGRAPHY LOG

DATE		TIME		○ AM ○ PM
IMAGE #				

SHOOTING MODE		METER MODE		
ISO		EV +/–		
WB		LENS		V R ○ ON ○ OFF
APERTURE		FOCAL LENGTH		
SHUTTER SPEED		FLASH	○ YES ○ NO	
TRIPOD	○ YES ○ NO	FLASH SETTINGS		

IN CAMERA SETTINGS	WEATHER

LIGHTING DESCRIPTION

PROPS USED	NOTES

PHOTOGRAPHY LOG

DATE		TIME		○ AM ○ PM
IMAGE #				

SHOOTING MODE		METER MODE		
ISO		EV +/−		
WB		LENS		V R ○ ON ○ OFF
APERTURE		FOCAL LENGTH		
SHUTTER SPEED		FLASH	○ YES ○ NO	
TRIPOD	○ YES ○ NO	FLASH SETTINGS		

IN CAMERA SETTINGS	WEATHER

LIGHTING DESCRIPTION

PROPS USED	NOTES

PHOTOGRAPHY LOG

DATE		TIME		○ AM ○ PM
IMAGE #				

SHOOTING MODE		METER MODE			
ISO		EV +/-			
WB		LENS		V R	○ ON ○ OFF
APERTURE		FOCAL LENGTH			
SHUTTER SPEED		FLASH	○ YES ○ NO		
TRIPOD	○ YES ○ NO	FLASH SETTINGS			

IN CAMERA SETTINGS	WEATHER

LIGHTING DESCRIPTION

PROPS USED	NOTES

PHOTOGRAPHY LOG

DATE		TIME		○ AM ○ PM
IMAGE #				

SHOOTING MODE		METER MODE	
ISO		EV +/-	
WB		LENS	V R ○ ON ○ OFF
APERTURE		FOCAL LENGTH	
SHUTTER SPEED		FLASH	○ YES ○ NO
TRIPOD	○ YES ○ NO	FLASH SETTINGS	

IN CAMERA SETTINGS	WEATHER

LIGHTING DESCRIPTION

PROPS USED	NOTES

PHOTOGRAPHY LOG

DATE		TIME		○ AM ○ PM
IMAGE #				

SHOOTING MODE		METER MODE	
ISO		EV +/-	
WB		LENS	V R — ○ ON ○ OFF
APERTURE		FOCAL LENGTH	
SHUTTER SPEED		FLASH	○ YES ○ NO
TRIPOD	○ YES ○ NO	FLASH SETTINGS	

IN CAMERA SETTINGS	WEATHER

LIGHTING DESCRIPTION

PROPS USED	NOTES

PHOTOGRAPHY LOG

DATE		TIME		○ AM ○ PM
IMAGE #				

SHOOTING MODE		METER MODE		
ISO		EV +/-		
WB		LENS		V R ○ ON ○ OFF
APERTURE		FOCAL LENGTH		
SHUTTER SPEED		FLASH	○ YES ○ NO	
TRIPOD	○ YES ○ NO	FLASH SETTINGS		

IN CAMERA SETTINGS	WEATHER

LIGHTING DESCRIPTION

PROPS USED	NOTES

PHOTOGRAPHY LOG

DATE		TIME		○ AM ○ PM
IMAGE #				

SHOOTING MODE		METER MODE	
ISO		EV +/-	
WB		LENS	V R ○ ON ○ OFF
APERTURE		FOCAL LENGTH	
SHUTTER SPEED		FLASH	○ YES ○ NO
TRIPOD	○ YES ○ NO	FLASH SETTINGS	

IN CAMERA SETTINGS	WEATHER

LIGHTING DESCRIPTION

PROPS USED	NOTES

PHOTOGRAPHY LOG

DATE		TIME		○ AM ○ PM
IMAGE #				

SHOOTING MODE		METER MODE		
ISO		EV +/-		
WB		LENS		V R ○ ON ○ OFF
APERTURE		FOCAL LENGTH		
SHUTTER SPEED		FLASH	○ YES ○ NO	
TRIPOD	○ YES ○ NO	FLASH SETTINGS		

IN CAMERA SETTINGS	WEATHER

LIGHTING DESCRIPTION

PROPS USED	NOTES

PHOTOGRAPHY LOG

DATE		TIME		○ AM ○ PM
IMAGE #				

SHOOTING MODE		METER MODE		
ISO		EV +/-		
WB		LENS		V R ○ ON ○ OFF
APERTURE		FOCAL LENGTH		
SHUTTER SPEED		FLASH	○ YES ○ NO	
TRIPOD	○ YES ○ NO	FLASH SETTINGS		

IN CAMERA SETTINGS	WEATHER

LIGHTING DESCRIPTION

PROPS USED	NOTES

PHOTOGRAPHY LOG

DATE		TIME		○ AM ○ PM
IMAGE #				

SHOOTING MODE		METER MODE		
ISO		EV +/-		
WB		LENS		V R	○ ON ○ OFF
APERTURE		FOCAL LENGTH		
SHUTTER SPEED		FLASH	○ YES ○ NO
TRIPOD	○ YES ○ NO	FLASH SETTINGS	

IN CAMERA SETTINGS	WEATHER

LIGHTING DESCRIPTION

PROPS USED	NOTES

PHOTOGRAPHY LOG

DATE		TIME		○ AM ○ PM
IMAGE #				

SHOOTING MODE		METER MODE	
ISO		EV +/-	
WB		LENS	V R ○ ON ○ OFF
APERTURE		FOCAL LENGTH	
SHUTTER SPEED		FLASH	○ YES ○ NO
TRIPOD	○ YES ○ NO	FLASH SETTINGS	

IN CAMERA SETTINGS	WEATHER

LIGHTING DESCRIPTION

PROPS USED	NOTES

PHOTOGRAPHY LOG

DATE		TIME		○ AM ○ PM
IMAGE #				

SHOOTING MODE		METER MODE		
ISO		EV +/-		
WB		LENS		V R ○ ON ○ OFF
APERTURE		FOCAL LENGTH		
SHUTTER SPEED		FLASH	○ YES ○ NO	
TRIPOD	○ YES ○ NO	FLASH SETTINGS		

IN CAMERA SETTINGS	WEATHER

LIGHTING DESCRIPTION

PROPS USED	NOTES

PHOTOGRAPHY LOG

DATE		TIME		○ AM ○ PM
IMAGE #				

SHOOTING MODE		METER MODE		
ISO		EV +/-		
WB		LENS		V R ○ ON ○ OFF
APERTURE		FOCAL LENGTH		
SHUTTER SPEED		FLASH	○ YES ○ NO	
TRIPOD	○ YES ○ NO	FLASH SETTINGS		

IN CAMERA SETTINGS	WEATHER

LIGHTING DESCRIPTION

PROPS USED	NOTES

PHOTOGRAPHY LOG

DATE		TIME		○ AM ○ PM
IMAGE #				

SHOOTING MODE		METER MODE	
ISO		EV +/-	
WB		LENS	V R — ○ ON ○ OFF
APERTURE		FOCAL LENGTH	
SHUTTER SPEED		FLASH	○ YES ○ NO
TRIPOD	○ YES ○ NO	FLASH SETTINGS	

IN CAMERA SETTINGS	WEATHER

LIGHTING DESCRIPTION

PROPS USED	NOTES

PHOTOGRAPHY LOG

DATE		TIME		○ AM ○ PM
IMAGE #				

SHOOTING MODE		METER MODE	
ISO		EV +/-	
WB		LENS		V R	○ ON ○ OFF
APERTURE		FOCAL LENGTH	
SHUTTER SPEED		FLASH	○ YES ○ NO
TRIPOD	○ YES ○ NO	FLASH SETTINGS	

IN CAMERA SETTINGS	WEATHER

LIGHTING DESCRIPTION

PROPS USED	NOTES

PHOTOGRAPHY LOG

DATE		TIME		○ AM ○ PM
IMAGE #				

SHOOTING MODE		METER MODE		
ISO		EV +/-		
WB		LENS		V R ○ ON ○ OFF
APERTURE		FOCAL LENGTH		
SHUTTER SPEED		FLASH	○ YES ○ NO	
TRIPOD	○ YES ○ NO	FLASH SETTINGS		

IN CAMERA SETTINGS	WEATHER

LIGHTING DESCRIPTION

PROPS USED	NOTES

PHOTOGRAPHY LOG

DATE		TIME		○ AM ○ PM
IMAGE #				

SHOOTING MODE		METER MODE		
ISO		EV +/–		
WB		LENS		V R ○ ON ○ OFF
APERTURE		FOCAL LENGTH		
SHUTTER SPEED		FLASH	○ YES ○ NO	
TRIPOD	○ YES ○ NO	FLASH SETTINGS		

IN CAMERA SETTINGS	WEATHER

LIGHTING DESCRIPTION

PROPS USED	NOTES

PHOTOGRAPHY LOG

DATE		TIME		○ AM ○ PM
IMAGE #				

SHOOTING MODE		METER MODE			
ISO		EV +/-			
WB		LENS		V R	○ ON ○ OFF
APERTURE		FOCAL LENGTH			
SHUTTER SPEED		FLASH	○ YES ○ NO		
TRIPOD	○ YES ○ NO	FLASH SETTINGS			

IN CAMERA SETTINGS	WEATHER

LIGHTING DESCRIPTION

PROPS USED	NOTES

PHOTOGRAPHY LOG

DATE		TIME		○ AM ○ PM
IMAGE #				

SHOOTING MODE		METER MODE	
ISO		EV +/-	
WB		LENS	V R ○ ON ○ OFF
APERTURE		FOCAL LENGTH	
SHUTTER SPEED		FLASH	○ YES ○ NO
TRIPOD	○ YES ○ NO	FLASH SETTINGS	

IN CAMERA SETTINGS	WEATHER

LIGHTING DESCRIPTION

PROPS USED	NOTES

PHOTOGRAPHY LOG

DATE		TIME		○ AM ○ PM
IMAGE #				

SHOOTING MODE		METER MODE	
ISO		EV +/-	
WB		LENS	V R ○ ON ○ OFF
APERTURE		FOCAL LENGTH	
SHUTTER SPEED		FLASH	○ YES ○ NO
TRIPOD	○ YES ○ NO	FLASH SETTINGS	

IN CAMERA SETTINGS	WEATHER

LIGHTING DESCRIPTION

PROPS USED	NOTES

PHOTOGRAPHY LOG

DATE		TIME		○ AM ○ PM
IMAGE #				

SHOOTING MODE		METER MODE			
ISO		EV +/-			
WB		LENS		V R	○ ON ○ OFF
APERTURE		FOCAL LENGTH			
SHUTTER SPEED		FLASH	○ YES ○ NO		
TRIPOD	○ YES ○ NO	FLASH SETTINGS			

IN CAMERA SETTINGS	WEATHER

LIGHTING DESCRIPTION

PROPS USED	NOTES

PHOTOGRAPHY LOG

DATE		TIME		○ AM ○ PM
IMAGE #				

SHOOTING MODE		METER MODE	
ISO		EV +/-	
WB		LENS	V R ○ ON ○ OFF
APERTURE		FOCAL LENGTH	
SHUTTER SPEED		FLASH	○ YES ○ NO
TRIPOD	○ YES ○ NO	FLASH SETTINGS	

IN CAMERA SETTINGS	WEATHER

LIGHTING DESCRIPTION

PROPS USED	NOTES

PHOTOGRAPHY LOG

DATE		TIME		○ AM ○ PM
IMAGE #				

SHOOTING MODE		METER MODE		
ISO		EV +/−		
WB		LENS		V R ○ ON ○ OFF
APERTURE		FOCAL LENGTH		
SHUTTER SPEED		FLASH	○ YES ○ NO	
TRIPOD	○ YES ○ NO	FLASH SETTINGS		

IN CAMERA SETTINGS	WEATHER

LIGHTING DESCRIPTION

PROPS USED	NOTES

PHOTOGRAPHY LOG

DATE		TIME		○ AM ○ PM
IMAGE #				

SHOOTING MODE		METER MODE		
ISO		EV +/-		
WB		LENS		V R ○ ON ○ OFF
APERTURE		FOCAL LENGTH		
SHUTTER SPEED		FLASH	○ YES ○ NO	
TRIPOD	○ YES ○ NO	FLASH SETTINGS		

IN CAMERA SETTINGS	WEATHER

LIGHTING DESCRIPTION

PROPS USED	NOTES

PHOTOGRAPHY LOG

DATE		TIME		○ AM ○ PM
IMAGE #				

SHOOTING MODE		METER MODE		
ISO		EV +/−		
WB		LENS		V R ○ ON ○ OFF
APERTURE		FOCAL LENGTH		
SHUTTER SPEED		FLASH	○ YES ○ NO	
TRIPOD	○ YES ○ NO	FLASH SETTINGS		

IN CAMERA SETTINGS	WEATHER

LIGHTING DESCRIPTION

PROPS USED	NOTES

PHOTOGRAPHY LOG

DATE		TIME		○ AM ○ PM
IMAGE #				

SHOOTING MODE		METER MODE		
ISO		EV +/-		
WB		LENS		V R ○ ON ○ OFF
APERTURE		FOCAL LENGTH		
SHUTTER SPEED		FLASH	○ YES ○ NO	
TRIPOD	○ YES ○ NO	FLASH SETTINGS		

IN CAMERA SETTINGS	WEATHER

LIGHTING DESCRIPTION

PROPS USED	NOTES

PHOTOGRAPHY LOG

DATE		TIME		○ AM ○ PM
IMAGE #				

SHOOTING MODE		METER MODE	
ISO		EV +/-	
WB		LENS	V R — ○ ON ○ OFF
APERTURE		FOCAL LENGTH	
SHUTTER SPEED		FLASH	○ YES ○ NO
TRIPOD	○ YES ○ NO	FLASH SETTINGS	

IN CAMERA SETTINGS	WEATHER

LIGHTING DESCRIPTION

PROPS USED	NOTES

PHOTOGRAPHY LOG

DATE		TIME		○ AM ○ PM
IMAGE #				

SHOOTING MODE		METER MODE	
ISO		EV +/−	
WB		LENS	V R ○ ON ○ OFF
APERTURE		FOCAL LENGTH	
SHUTTER SPEED		FLASH	○ YES ○ NO
TRIPOD	○ YES ○ NO	FLASH SETTINGS	

IN CAMERA SETTINGS	WEATHER

LIGHTING DESCRIPTION

PROPS USED	NOTES

PHOTOGRAPHY LOG

DATE		TIME		○ AM ○ PM
IMAGE #				

SHOOTING MODE		METER MODE	
ISO		EV +/−	
WB		LENS	V R ○ ON ○ OFF
APERTURE		FOCAL LENGTH	
SHUTTER SPEED		FLASH	○ YES ○ NO
TRIPOD	○ YES ○ NO	FLASH SETTINGS	

IN CAMERA SETTINGS	WEATHER

LIGHTING DESCRIPTION

PROPS USED	NOTES

PHOTOGRAPHY LOG

DATE		TIME		○ AM ○ PM
IMAGE #				

SHOOTING MODE		METER MODE	
ISO		EV +/-	
WB		LENS	V R ○ ON ○ OFF
APERTURE		FOCAL LENGTH	
SHUTTER SPEED		FLASH	○ YES ○ NO
TRIPOD	○ YES ○ NO	FLASH SETTINGS	

IN CAMERA SETTINGS	WEATHER

LIGHTING DESCRIPTION

PROPS USED	NOTES

PHOTOGRAPHY LOG

DATE		TIME		○ AM ○ PM
IMAGE #				

SHOOTING MODE		METER MODE	
ISO		EV +/−	
WB		LENS	V R ○ ON ○ OFF
APERTURE		FOCAL LENGTH	
SHUTTER SPEED		FLASH	○ YES ○ NO
TRIPOD	○ YES ○ NO	FLASH SETTINGS	

IN CAMERA SETTINGS	WEATHER

LIGHTING DESCRIPTION

PROPS USED	NOTES

PHOTOGRAPHY LOG

DATE		TIME		○ AM ○ PM
IMAGE #				

SHOOTING MODE		METER MODE	
ISO		EV +/-	
WB		LENS	V R ○ ON ○ OFF
APERTURE		FOCAL LENGTH	
SHUTTER SPEED		FLASH	○ YES ○ NO
TRIPOD	○ YES ○ NO	FLASH SETTINGS	

IN CAMERA SETTINGS	WEATHER

LIGHTING DESCRIPTION

PROPS USED	NOTES

PHOTOGRAPHY LOG

DATE		TIME		○ AM ○ PM
IMAGE #				

SHOOTING MODE		METER MODE	
ISO		EV +/-	
WB		LENS	V R ○ ON ○ OFF
APERTURE		FOCAL LENGTH	
SHUTTER SPEED		FLASH	○ YES ○ NO
TRIPOD	○ YES ○ NO	FLASH SETTINGS	

IN CAMERA SETTINGS	WEATHER

LIGHTING DESCRIPTION

PROPS USED	NOTES

PHOTOGRAPHY LOG

DATE		TIME		○ AM ○ PM
IMAGE #				

SHOOTING MODE		METER MODE		
ISO		EV +/−		
WB		LENS		V R ○ ON ○ OFF
APERTURE		FOCAL LENGTH		
SHUTTER SPEED		FLASH	○ YES ○ NO	
TRIPOD	○ YES ○ NO	FLASH SETTINGS		

IN CAMERA SETTINGS	WEATHER

LIGHTING DESCRIPTION

PROPS USED	NOTES

PHOTOGRAPHY LOG

DATE		TIME		○ AM ○ PM
IMAGE #				

SHOOTING MODE		METER MODE		
ISO		EV +/-		
WB		LENS		V R ○ ON ○ OFF
APERTURE		FOCAL LENGTH		
SHUTTER SPEED		FLASH	○ YES ○ NO	
TRIPOD	○ YES ○ NO	FLASH SETTINGS		

IN CAMERA SETTINGS	WEATHER

LIGHTING DESCRIPTION

PROPS USED	NOTES

PHOTOGRAPHY LOG

DATE		TIME		○ AM ○ PM
IMAGE #				

SHOOTING MODE		METER MODE	
ISO		EV +/-	
WB		LENS	V R ○ ON ○ OFF
APERTURE		FOCAL LENGTH	
SHUTTER SPEED		FLASH	○ YES ○ NO
TRIPOD	○ YES ○ NO	FLASH SETTINGS	

IN CAMERA SETTINGS	WEATHER

LIGHTING DESCRIPTION

PROPS USED	NOTES

PHOTOGRAPHY LOG

DATE		TIME		○ AM ○ PM
IMAGE #				

SHOOTING MODE		METER MODE		
ISO		EV +/-		
WB		LENS		V R ○ ON ○ OFF
APERTURE		FOCAL LENGTH		
SHUTTER SPEED		FLASH	○ YES ○ NO	
TRIPOD	○ YES ○ NO	FLASH SETTINGS		

IN CAMERA SETTINGS	WEATHER

LIGHTING DESCRIPTION

PROPS USED	NOTES

PHOTOGRAPHY LOG

DATE		TIME		○ AM ○ PM
IMAGE #				

SHOOTING MODE		METER MODE		
ISO		EV +/−		
WB		LENS		V R ○ ON ○ OFF
APERTURE		FOCAL LENGTH		
SHUTTER SPEED		FLASH	○ YES ○ NO	
TRIPOD	○ YES ○ NO	FLASH SETTINGS		

IN CAMERA SETTINGS	WEATHER

LIGHTING DESCRIPTION

PROPS USED	NOTES

PHOTOGRAPHY LOG

DATE		TIME		○ AM ○ PM
IMAGE #				

SHOOTING MODE		METER MODE		
ISO		EV +/-		
WB		LENS		V R ○ ON ○ OFF
APERTURE		FOCAL LENGTH		
SHUTTER SPEED		FLASH	○ YES ○ NO	
TRIPOD	○ YES ○ NO	FLASH SETTINGS		

IN CAMERA SETTINGS	WEATHER

LIGHTING DESCRIPTION

PROPS USED	NOTES

PHOTOGRAPHY LOG

DATE		TIME		○ AM ○ PM
IMAGE #				

SHOOTING MODE		METER MODE		
ISO		EV +/-		
WB		LENS		V R ○ ON ○ OFF
APERTURE		FOCAL LENGTH		
SHUTTER SPEED		FLASH	○ YES ○ NO	
TRIPOD	○ YES ○ NO	FLASH SETTINGS		

IN CAMERA SETTINGS	WEATHER

LIGHTING DESCRIPTION

PROPS USED	NOTES

PHOTOGRAPHY LOG

DATE		TIME		○ AM ○ PM
IMAGE #				

SHOOTING MODE		METER MODE	
ISO		EV +/-	
WB		LENS	V R — ○ ON ○ OFF
APERTURE		FOCAL LENGTH	
SHUTTER SPEED		FLASH	○ YES ○ NO
TRIPOD	○ YES ○ NO	FLASH SETTINGS	

IN CAMERA SETTINGS	WEATHER

LIGHTING DESCRIPTION

PROPS USED	NOTES

PHOTOGRAPHY LOG

DATE		TIME		○ AM ○ PM
IMAGE #				

SHOOTING MODE		METER MODE		
ISO		EV +/-		
WB		LENS		V R ○ ON ○ OFF
APERTURE		FOCAL LENGTH		
SHUTTER SPEED		FLASH	○ YES ○ NO	
TRIPOD	○ YES ○ NO	FLASH SETTINGS		

IN CAMERA SETTINGS	WEATHER

LIGHTING DESCRIPTION

PROPS USED	NOTES

PHOTOGRAPHY LOG

DATE		TIME		○ AM ○ PM
IMAGE #				

SHOOTING MODE		METER MODE		
ISO		EV +/-		
WB		LENS		V R ○ ON ○ OFF
APERTURE		FOCAL LENGTH		
SHUTTER SPEED		FLASH	○ YES ○ NO	
TRIPOD	○ YES ○ NO	FLASH SETTINGS		

IN CAMERA SETTINGS	WEATHER

LIGHTING DESCRIPTION

PROPS USED	NOTES

PHOTOGRAPHY LOG

DATE		TIME		○ AM ○ PM
IMAGE #				

SHOOTING MODE		METER MODE		
ISO		EV +/-		
WB		LENS		V R ○ ON ○ OFF
APERTURE		FOCAL LENGTH		
SHUTTER SPEED		FLASH	○ YES ○ NO	
TRIPOD	○ YES ○ NO	FLASH SETTINGS		

IN CAMERA SETTINGS	WEATHER

LIGHTING DESCRIPTION

PROPS USED	NOTES

PHOTOGRAPHY LOG

DATE		TIME		○ AM ○ PM
IMAGE #				

SHOOTING MODE		METER MODE	
ISO		EV +/-	
WB		LENS	V R ○ ON ○ OFF
APERTURE		FOCAL LENGTH	
SHUTTER SPEED		FLASH	○ YES ○ NO
TRIPOD	○ YES ○ NO	FLASH SETTINGS	

IN CAMERA SETTINGS	WEATHER

LIGHTING DESCRIPTION

PROPS USED	NOTES

PHOTOGRAPHY LOG

DATE		TIME		○ AM ○ PM
IMAGE #				

SHOOTING MODE		METER MODE	
ISO		EV +/-	
WB		LENS	V R ○ ON ○ OFF
APERTURE		FOCAL LENGTH	
SHUTTER SPEED		FLASH	○ YES ○ NO
TRIPOD	○ YES ○ NO	FLASH SETTINGS	

IN CAMERA SETTINGS	WEATHER

LIGHTING DESCRIPTION

PROPS USED	NOTES

PHOTOGRAPHY LOG

DATE		TIME		○ AM ○ PM
IMAGE #				

SHOOTING MODE		METER MODE		
ISO		EV +/-		
WB		LENS		V R ○ ON ○OFF
APERTURE		FOCAL LENGTH		
SHUTTER SPEED		FLASH	○ YES ○ NO	
TRIPOD	○ YES ○ NO	FLASH SETTINGS		

IN CAMERA SETTINGS	WEATHER

LIGHTING DESCRIPTION

PROPS USED	NOTES

PHOTOGRAPHY LOG

DATE		TIME		○ AM ○ PM
IMAGE #				

SHOOTING MODE		METER MODE	
ISO		EV +/-	
WB		LENS	V R ○ ON ○ OFF
APERTURE		FOCAL LENGTH	
SHUTTER SPEED		FLASH	○ YES ○ NO
TRIPOD	○ YES ○ NO	FLASH SETTINGS	

IN CAMERA SETTINGS	WEATHER

LIGHTING DESCRIPTION

PROPS USED	NOTES

PHOTOGRAPHY LOG

DATE		TIME		○ AM ○ PM
IMAGE #				

SHOOTING MODE		METER MODE	
ISO		EV +/-	
WB		LENS	V R ○ ON ○ OFF
APERTURE		FOCAL LENGTH	
SHUTTER SPEED		FLASH	○ YES ○ NO
TRIPOD	○ YES ○ NO	FLASH SETTINGS	

IN CAMERA SETTINGS	WEATHER

LIGHTING DESCRIPTION

PROPS USED	NOTES

PHOTOGRAPHY LOG

DATE		TIME		○ AM ○ PM
IMAGE #				

SHOOTING MODE		METER MODE		
ISO		EV +/-		
WB		LENS	V R	○ ON ○ OFF
APERTURE		FOCAL LENGTH		
SHUTTER SPEED		FLASH	○ YES ○ NO	
TRIPOD	○ YES ○ NO	FLASH SETTINGS		

IN CAMERA SETTINGS	WEATHER

LIGHTING DESCRIPTION

PROPS USED	NOTES

PHOTOGRAPHY LOG

DATE		TIME		○ AM ○ PM
IMAGE #				

SHOOTING MODE		METER MODE		
ISO		EV +/−		
WB		LENS		V R ○ ON ○ OFF
APERTURE		FOCAL LENGTH		
SHUTTER SPEED		FLASH	○ YES ○ NO	
TRIPOD	○ YES ○ NO	FLASH SETTINGS		

IN CAMERA SETTINGS	WEATHER

LIGHTING DESCRIPTION

PROPS USED	NOTES

PHOTOGRAPHY LOG

DATE		TIME		○ AM ○ PM
IMAGE #				

SHOOTING MODE		METER MODE	
ISO		EV +/-	
WB		LENS	V R ○ ON ○ OFF
APERTURE		FOCAL LENGTH	
SHUTTER SPEED		FLASH	○ YES ○ NO
TRIPOD	○ YES ○ NO	FLASH SETTINGS	

IN CAMERA SETTINGS	WEATHER

LIGHTING DESCRIPTION

PROPS USED	NOTES

www.ingramcontent.com/pod-product-compliance
Lightning Source LLC
Chambersburg PA
CBHW051506050726
47593CB00005B/2245